YOUR KNOWLEDGE HAS VALUE

- We will publish your bachelor's and
  master's thesis, essays and papers

- Your own eBook and book -
  sold worldwide in all relevant shops

- Earn money with each sale

Upload your text at www.GRIN.com
and publish for free

Viola Abelius

PENOLOGY. Critically Assessment of the Suggestion that Prisons have moved on little from the Concerns raised in John Howard's Famous Statement of 1777

With Reference to the Current Crisis of Prison Numbers

GRIN Verlag

Bibliografische Information der Deutschen Nationalbibliothek:

Die Deutsche Bibliothek verzeichnet diese Publikation in der Deutschen National-
bibliografie; detaillierte bibliografische Daten sind im Internet über http://dnb.d-
nb.de/ abrufbar.

Imprint:

Copyright © 2008 GRIN Verlag GmbH
Druck und Bindung: Books on Demand GmbH, Norderstedt Germany
ISBN: 978-3-656-48302-1

This book at GRIN:

http://www.grin.com/en/e-book/180881/penology-critically-assessment-of-the-sug-
gestion-that-prisons-have-moved

PENOLOGY

With Reference to the Current Crisis of Prison Numbers, Critically Assess the Suggestion that Prisons have moved on little from the Concerns raised in John Howard's Famous Statement of 1777.

When politician and prison reformer John Howard 1777 called prisons 'filthy and corrupt-ridden places, not fit for human habitation', he surely had no idea how much truth still would be in his words and how much this would still be an issue in the 21st century. This critique shall show the prison history from the late 18th century until today with special emphasis on the state and condition of the prisons and resulting from this the situation of the prisoners at that time within the prisons and the penal system.

John Howard (1726 – 1790), politician and prison reformer in late 18th century, was shocked by the unbearable conditions within the custodial institutions in England, which he got to know during his time as supervisor of the Bedfordshire county jail where he was appointed High Sheriff in the 1750's. Alarmed by the horrible conditions there, he visited different prisons all over the country and decided to ameliorate the terrible situation the prisoners had to suffer during their incarceration. (BBC Homepage, 2008). Amongst others, prisoners had to pay the jailers for food, bedding, etc. as the jailers did not get any salaries from the state. Resulting from this, the living conditions for the prisoners were so bad that they sometimes had to stay in prison even if they were innocent or their sentence was already served just because they could not pay enough money to the jailers (The Howard League for Penal Reform, 2006; BBC, 2008).

This fact made poorer prisoners suffer longer than the ones who had more financial possibilities - a fact which is mirrored still today in penal custody, for example regarding fines for less serious delinquencies which cannot be paid and finally result in a prison sentence. To give some more examples of prison life in the 18th century, "The State of the Prisons" written by John Howard and first published in 1777, provides an excellent, if not the best, source of material in this field of research.

Key words of incarceration at this period in history can easily give us an impression of how it must have been to be a prisoner at this time: Howard speaks of a great error in the management of prisons, of miserable conditions, of diseases like pestilential fever or smallpox. He blames the officials, namely the sheriffs and gentlemen in the commission of peace, of cruelty and inattention. (Muncie, Sparks, 1991, p. 7-11).

Besides the work of Howard, a very close and well-reported insight view into prison life of the 18th century is presented by Cesare Beccaria (1738 – 1794) and by Michel Foucault (1926 – 1984). Beccaria, for instance, describes in 'On crimes and punishments' the situation in penal institutions of the 18th century as a situation, where the severity of punishment drives men to additional crimes to avoid the punishment for a single one (Beccaria, 1764/1963, p.43). Taking a look to the United States, one could argue to find an equivalent there in regard of the capital punishment, which too often seems to give an explanation for serial killings or the enormous cruelty of some cases of capital crimes, as if the perpetrators would think – why should I only kill one person and get the death penalty, when I can kill five more and get the same punishment? It does not matter for them, as it does not make any difference in the consequence of their deeds.

Beccaria talks about 'keeping the proportion' in punishment (p.42), which means that the crimes committed should be punished in a reasonable and appropriate way, a theory, which we nowadays know as bifurcation (Cavadino, Dignan, 2007, p.399). In 'Discipline & Punish', Foucault describes in full length the ways of public torturing and public killings in the 18th and 19th century (Foucault, 1975/1995, p.3-14); the last public hanging had been carried out in 1868. The only Western "civilized" country, in which a form of public killing still is performed, are the USA when executing their death row prisoners under the eyes of relatives and officials or even with television broadcast, the height of perversity is reached. Foucault puts it in the best possible way saying, that the death penalty in prisons occupied the place left vacant by the disappearance of public torture (p.117) – so how far away are we from 1777? In 1965, the death penalty had been abolished in the U.K. finally. But, despite all political correctness and policy of humanity, still today, torture is a means to extort confessions from suspects, while the only difference is, the torture or, call it police violence, is no *official* method any more, but tolerated anyway.

Additionally to torture, diseases, denial of bedding, food or even water and clean air, another grave problem was the mental state of the prisoners. At Howard's time, mental care for prisoners was not on the agenda, a lot of suicide incidents occurred and mentally insane prisoners were kept like everybody else like animals in cages behind the prison bars. In 1784, Howard traces the situation of mentally ill prisoners back to the overcrowded and like he calls them 'offensive' prisons, where no care is taken of the mentally ill, although some of them might be lead back to a certain usefulness in their lives if medicated in the right way (Reed, 2003).

With his incessant engagement, Howard reached the requirement for all prisons to constitute a surgeon or a apothecary in 1774, but still today regarding mental health problems of prisoners, court assessments are inadequate and offer too few psychiatric beds or mental help to prisoners in need, and furthermore, they give too often poor identification during reception into prison (Reed, 2003).

Former Chief Inspector or Prisons (1995-2001), David Ramsbotham, reports about the horrible state of British prisons today. After he had carried out an unannounced inspection of HM Prison Holloway in 1995, he was shocked by the unbearable conditions in this penal institution, which he describes in his book as 'filthy' (Ramsbotham, 2003, p. 5), like a two hundred years before Howard named the state of British prisons. He also confirms Howard's observations, when he describes the way prisoners are treated, locked up all day, doing nothing (compare Howard in Muncie and Sparks, 1991, p.8), being victims of extreme bullying, not receiving appropriate food at correct times (Ramsbotham, 2003, p. 1-2 & 6-7).

So, how far have we moved on until today within penal policy and imprisonment in particular? To answer this is the aim of this essay, an answer which requires the direct comparison of the specifically addressed problems in prison's daily life by John Howard's speech of 1777 to the situations and states of prisons in the U.K. nowadays.

Howard speaks of 'filthy and corrupt-ridden places, not fit for human habitation', a statement which addresses different aspects, like the aspect of hygiene, the political and finally the humane aspect in terms of a fair treatment of the prison inmates.

First of all, we will try to present some facts about the state of hygiene, medical support and diseases in prisons today. The Dictionary of Prisons and Punishment (Jewkes and Bennett, 2008) calls prisons 'a key setting for the transmission of multiple infections, such as HIV, tuberculosis, Hepatitis C, or other sexually transmitted infections. The rates of HIV as well as Hepatitis C in prisons is significantly higher than in the general population, which expressed in numbers means a 15-times-higher rate of HIV and even a 20-times-higher rate of Hepatitis C. Wide-spread drug-misuse in prisons additionally aggravates the circumstances and the risk of infections. Besides drug-abuse and sexual abuse, alcoholism contributes to early deaths within prison and to mental health problems throughout the prison population, as already mentioned above. Mental health care today is on the agenda in prisons, but the quality of this care must be called in question, though. According to Reed, the first full survey of the mental health of prisoners in England and Wales (1997 undertaken by ONS, Office for National Statistics, emerged 1996) showed that the prevalence of mental health problems was much higher in prison population than among the general population, which means in numbers, only one prisoner in ten showed no evidence of mental disorder, respectively, over 90 per cent had one or more psychiatric disorder (Reed, 2003 and Jewkes & Bennett, 2008). A strong evidence of mental disorders in prisons, which arise from drug abuse, isolation, sexual abuse and so on, are the suicide rates among the prison population: the Prison Reform Trust published an average rate of one in five male prisoners that are on prescribed medication, such as anti-depressants, and also one in five male prisoners attempting suicide. The suicide rates of women are even higher. The problem of mental disorder in prisons is mainly a problem of untrained staff being overcharged with this burden and the result often is an increase of prescribed anti-psychotic medicine (Prison Reform Trust, 2004 & 2005). To cite one more figure – during 2004, 95 people killed themselves in prison service care and in 2003, 30% of women, 65% of females under 21 and 6% of men in prison harmed themselves (The Howard League for Penal Reform, 2006).

Looking at the issue of corruption and bribery, John Howard spoke about in his famous speech, we have to admit that this, too, is no problem solely of the past. As we learned from John Howard, in the 18th century, the prison guards had to be bribed to enable the accused a bearable prison sentence. And, although, today's prison guards do have a regular income – opposite to former times – corruption is still a part of prison life today. Hope cites a report commissioned by Secretary of State for Justice Jack Straw, which comes to the conclusion, that the drug smuggling within British prisons was possible to a great part by the help of corrupt prison employees (Hope, 2008). Confirming these findings, Purdy figures a number of more than 1,000 police officers, who are allegedly involved in corruption (Purdy, 2006).

An interesting finding was identified with the interviewing of prisoners in different penal institutions within the scope of the Home Office's 'Measuring the quality of prison life': the proportion of safety and of respect towards the prisoners was opposite, which means, that if prisoners felt safe within a penal institution, the feeling of respect always was low, and if they felt respected the feeling of safety was not satisfying (HO, 2002). Perhaps the most meaningful attempt to an enduring prison reform in our times was the *Woolf Report* of 1991, in which Lord Chief Justice Woolf criticised inhumane prison conditions and promoted a balance between security, control, and justice, but in the end it remained an attempt as with the new Home Secretary John Reid the construction of further prison places was announced in 2006 describing the managerial crisis in the penal system (Cavadino & Dignan, 2007, p.202-203 and Scott, 2008, p.69).

As a conclusion we can say, that prison today in many aspects has moved on very little from the situation in the late 18th century. Similar problems like then, like corrupt prison staff, untrained and insufficient staff unable to respond to the needs of prisoners in regards of health, mental health, useful occupation, or the care for their lives still exist to a huge extent. The main differences are, that opposite to then, today a penal policy in favour of prisoners exists – on the paper – and the failures of penal policy, which make such horrible living conditions within prisons possible, are not the norm, but they are reality, still, and might make prisoners feel the horror of being in prison in 1777. Besides such problems like the lack of hygiene, which leads to a lack of clean needles for drug-addicts, and thus leads to HIV or Hepatitis C, a high rate of suicides, self-harm-incidents, or even murderers within prison makes them no good places to be, still today. Despite good plans for prison reforms, such as the *Woolf Report* of 1991, the crisis of penal policy with overcrowded prisons seems to go on unstoppable. One could argue, that 200 years after prison reformer John Howard fought for the first medical care and better living conditions in England's penal institutions, the prison reform yet is unfinished.

References

Beccaria, C. (1764; edition of 1963). *On Crimes and Punishment.* New Jersey, USA: Prentice-Hall Inc.

BBC Homepage (2008). *Historic Figures: John Howard* (BBC History). Retrieved July 31, 2008 from the BBC- Homepage: http://www.bbc.co.uk/history/historic_figures/howard_john.shtml

Cavadino, M. and Dignan, J. (2007). *The Penal System. An Introduction. Fourth Edition.* London, UK: Sage Publications Ltd.

Foucault, M. (1975, edition of 1995). *Discipline & Punish. The Birth of the Prison.* New York, USA: Vintage Books.

Home Office. Great Britain. (2002). Findings 174. *Measuring the quality of prison life.* London: HMSO.

Hope, C. (2008, July 08). Corrupt prison guards fuel drug culture [Electronic Version]. Retrieved October 29, 2008 from the Telegraph- Homepage: http://www.telegraph.co.uk/news/newstopics/politics/lawandorder/2262984/'Corrupt'-prison-guards-fuel-drug-culture-in-prison.html

The Howard League For Penal Reform (2006). *John Howard & The History of the Howard League For Penal Reform.* Retrieved August 23, 2008 from the Howard League- Homepage: http://www.howardleague.org/

Jewkes, Y. and Bennett, J. (2008). *Dictionary of Prisons and Punishment.* Cullompton, UK: Willan Publishing.

Muncie, J., Sparks, R. (1991). *Imprisonment. European Perspectives.* London, UK: Harvester Wheatsheaf. The Open University.

Office for National Statistics (ONS, 2008). *Our History.* Retrieved from the ONS-Homepage: http://www.ons.gov.uk/about

The Prison Reform Trust (2004). *Mental Health Crisis Among Male Prisoners.* Retrieved October 22, 2008 from the Prison Reform Trust-Homepage: http://www.prisonreformtrust.org.uk/subsection.asp?id=317

The Prison Reform Trust (2005). *Troubled Inside: Mental Health Care In Prisons.* Retrieved October 13, 2008 from the Prison Reform Trust-Homepage: http://www.prisonreformtrust.org.uk/subsection.asp?id=438

Purdy, A. (2006, July 31). *Prison Service 'institutionally corrupt'* [Electronic Version]. Retrieved October 29, 2008 from the Independent- Homepage: http://www.independent.co.uk/news/uk/crime/prison-service-institutionally-corrupt-410046.html

Ramsbotham, D. (2003). Prisongate. *The Shocking State of Britain's Prisons and the Need for Visionary Change.* London: The Free Press.

Reed, J. (2003). Mental health care in prisons [Electronic Version]. *The British Journal of Psychiatry, 182,* p. 287-288.

Scott, D. (2008). *Sage Course Companions: Penology.* London, UK: Sage Publications Ltd.